Who Packed My Baggage?

Who Packed My Baggage?

A Fun Six-Step Approach To Managing Change In Work And Life

Cat Langdon

iUniverse, Inc.

New York Lincoln Shanghai

Who Packed My Baggage?
A Fun Six-Step Approach To Managing Change In Work And Life

All Rights Reserved © 2004 by Cat Langdon

iUniverse, Inc.

For information address:
iUniverse, Inc.
2021 Pine Lake Road, Suite 100
Lincoln, NE 68512
www.iuniverse.com

ISBN: 0-595-31449-X

Printed in the United States of America

"The voyage of discovery is not in seeking new landscapes but in new eyes."

—Marcel Proust

I dedicate this book to my daughter Hayley.

Contents

Acknowledgement

I give special thanks to my friend, anchor, and Inspire Communications Unlimited Co-founder, Liz Forbes, for her exceptional support in the editing and preparation of this project. I wish to acknowledge Joanne Klassen, for her Heart Space Transformative Process™ where *Who Packed My Baggage?* was born. To my Reflective Hearts mates: Krista, Martha, Linda, David, Cyn, and Leslie, I am grateful to belong to such an inspiring and talented group of writers and friends. Thank you for the many thoughtful "seeds" and "power notes." My heartfelt gratitude to the many talented leaders, friends, peers and teachers I've had the opportunity to share with and learn from over the years. Many thanks to my brother Rob for his assistance with the cover design.

Foreword

Just last night I caught myself thinking, "I'm happy with my life the way it is. I don't want anything to change. What if I don't like what's going to happen next?" Thankfully, I have an easy step-by-step way to work through my concerns. It's not going to change the fact that there's going to be change. What it does affect is how we can feel about change and how to take care of ourselves. We can have a level of control and make the best decisions for ourselves, no matter what else may be happening around us. *Who Packed My Baggage?* is a practical six-step process that has been developed by Cat Langdon, applied to various situations, and it works. I invite you to turn the page and find out how *Who Packed My Baggage?* can work for you.

Liz Forbes, Co-founder
Inspire Communications Unlimited

Experience *Who Packed My Baggage?*

What you can expect from your *Who Packed My Baggage?* experience:

Objectives:

- Expand knowledge and understanding of change

- Facilitate personal and professional growth

- Promote personal "ownership" of the change experience

- Increase confidence and self-esteem

- Increase personal and/or job satisfaction

- Encourage teamwork and leadership

- Promote a positive environment for change

- Improve morale

- Increase ability to deal with change

- Increase acceptance of change

- Empowerment

Benefits:

- Appeals to many learning styles

- Stimulates the senses

- Practical to apply

- Easy to understand

- Promotes learning through play and fun

- Motivates continuous learning

Applications:

- Behavior

- Attitudes

- Confidence

- Self-esteem

- Knowledge

- Morale

Introduction

Every time I check in at an airport, the agent at the customer service counter asks me, "Did you pack your own baggage?"

"Yes, I did," I answer with certainty. "Did you leave it unattended at any time?" the agent prods. "I did not," I respond seriously. "Has anyone else had access to your baggage?" "Just me," I smile proudly, "I packed it all myself."

The agent nods approvingly and my bags are tagged. I wait patiently while each one is placed on a scale. The agent shakes her head and clucks her tongue, "I'm sorry Ms. Langdon. Your baggage is over the weight and size limit. It will cost an additional $50 for each bag."

What? My mind and body race with thoughts and feelings. How could this happen to me? I can't afford another penny for this trip. I need everything that's inside my bags. I packed the way I always do.

"What's different this time?" I ask wide-eyed.

"Well," she pauses, "If you had checked your ticket, you would know that this trip is destined for *'Change'*. I'm afraid you'll either have to pay the penalty for your excess baggage or pack again. The choice is yours. By the way, this is the last boarding call. The plane will be leaving in 10 minutes."

A bead of sweat begins to form on my brow. My collar suddenly tightens around my neck, my heart pounds frantically in my chest. I search the agent's face for an answer. She glances at her watch and waits expectantly for my decision.

What would you do?

Chapter 1

Who Packed My Baggage?

Life has a way of throwing you twists and turns with little regard for your best laid plans. Many times, situations go much differently than you expect and changes that you never thought would happen suddenly come knocking uninvited at your door. You have picked up this book because you are ready to learn a new way to deal with life's surprises. *Who Packed My Baggage?* takes you through six easy steps to manage change:

Step 1 **Check Your Ticket**
Name your destination, situation or problem

Step 2 **Pack Your Baggage**
Identify your thoughts, feelings and beliefs

Step 3 **Claim Your Lost Baggage**
Consider your other options

Step 4 **Choose Your Fare**
Decide where to put your energy and resources

Step 5 **Make Your Connections**
Find your opportunities for learning and growth

Step 6 **Arrive At Your Destination**
Own your outcome

From checking your ticket and naming your destination, situation, or problem to arriving at your destination and owning your outcome, you will become more effective and confident in dealing with change.

Each step is important to realize the full benefits of managing change. It may be as simple as answering the question, "How do I decide what to do on my day off?" to as grand as a life altering experience like, "How do I change my career or my relationship?" *Who Packed My Baggage?* will provide you with a travel bag full of tools to evaluate your goals and make wise choices, keeping you on the most positive path of change and bringing you the success and personal power you desire. The energy you give and the fare you choose is entirely up to you.

There is only one very important and necessary restriction to your travel that will ensure your comfort and safety during the journey. The restriction states:

My Ticket Restriction

Through the course of my journey, I understand and agree that there will be no putting down, no berating, no judgment, and no criticism of myself or anyone else in any way, shape or form. Liability for loss, delay or damage to my baggage is limited to the price I am willing to pay. This ticket is good for life.

This is your invitation to explore your understanding, attitudes, motivation, and choices around an area that will never change...*Change.* There is no obligation or expectation that you take this journey. Just know that once you've booked your ticket for change, you can learn how to take care of yourself, manage your attitude, take ownership, choose your battles, be tolerant, be committed, be responsible, support others, and invest in your future. The sky is the limit.

Chapter 2

The Travel Question

Managing change in your work and your life is almost the same as going on a trip. You can strategize and plan, decide where to go, who to travel with, how much time and resources to invest, and prepare for the unexpected. You may wait until the last minute, grab your toothbrush, shampoo, and deodorant; gather a few pieces of clothing that are clean (or at least not too wrinkled), your wallet, and a pack of gum, throw them into a travel bag and head to the airport. This can be thrilling, until you arrive to check in only to realize that you've left your ticket on the kitchen counter. You find out that contrary to your belief, you don't have a first class seat assignment. In fact, you have no seat assignment and how does 32C at the very back beside the toilets sound? After berating yourself for your oversights, your next stop is the customs official who thinks you look disheveled and harried and perhaps a few choice questions are in order. You wonder what else could possibly happen?

Changes in your life may often feel this way: unanticipated, inconvenient, and unwanted. Since traveling through life is the most important journey you will take, it makes sense to give it your attention. Depending on how you pack, your trip can be bumpy and make you sick, or smooth sailing all the way.

Why are we in constant flux? Why can't things just remain the same? We will always be driven by change because we live in a dynamic world. People, ideas, relationships, technology, business, information, understanding, and knowledge are forever changing. Being able to manage the journey of change is a valuable skill that you will find yourself using time and time again.

We all know what it's like to prepare and pack for a trip. There are so many things to remember and so many things to do. You want to be absolutely sure that you don't leave anything important behind. As you pack for a trip you may have many questions. What is essential to take with you on this trip? What will the weather be like? What personal items will you need? Will you need one travel bag or three? What do you need to shop for before leaving? What can you pick up along the way? Will you want a book or magazine to read?

When you take your journey of change, you will have to think about what you will take along with you, what you can leave behind, and how you will get to your destination emotionally, physically, intellectually and spiritually.

What if the trip is bumpy or you become dehydrated? Maybe motion sickness medication or cold water would be a good idea. Snacks. You better take snacks in case no one feeds you. What if you forget something? What if you don't know something? Where are the washrooms? Will you make all your connections at each destination? What if they lose your baggage? You may want to call it quits before you even get started.

You will have to consider what you will do if your journey through change is uncomfortable. What does the change mean to you? What resources and support systems will you have in place? Where is the best place to put your energy? How can you prevent burnout? What will you need to learn? What do you need to focus on for results? How can you manage your stress and emotions? What's important and what's not?

How do you get through it all? How can you be sure you are ready for your trip (a job change, a relationship, new skills, lifestyle)? Wouldn't it be grand to avoid a confrontation with the customer service agent (your boss, your spouse, a sibling, a friend, a co-worker)? There is a lot to think about when your destination is "Change."

You can build a framework to rely upon in any situation to guide you in rapidly assimilating and accepting any change. Life is a journey with endless situations which may at first feel challenging and even painful but ultimately lead to progress, gain, and success. You are here for a reason and this is the perfect moment to choose how to travel.

Chapter 3

Step 1: Check Your Ticket

To begin designing your itinerary for change, the first step is to name your destination. This means you need to describe your situation, question, problem, or the issue facing you. Whether change finds you or you seek change, clearly knowing the nature of your problem or issue will make it easier to plan the itinerary for the rest of your journey.

You may need or want to go on a journey to bring about change in any of the many facets of your life—physically, emotionally, spiritually, professionally, financially, or intellectually. You may want or need to improve your skills or education to keep up with ever changing business needs. Your physical or emotional well-being may be in need of repair. Relationships with yourself and others in your life may no longer be fulfilling or may be dysfunctional. The organization you work with or your career may be in transition.

These are only some of the situations that may evolve during the course of your already busy life. Such changes are not always so polite as to ask whether they may come in, or arrive one at a time. Life changes may barge right in, unannounced, to greet you enthusiastically en masse. Many times change is imposed upon you, and if you had a preference, you may choose not to participate. Often, you have no choice.

I recall a time a few years ago when my friend Carol was living an enviable life. She boasted a handsome husband, a new baby, a fabulous job, an active social life, a beautiful home, a cottage at the lake, and more. Without any obvious warning to family, friends, and most importantly to her, life as she knew it took a dramatic and unexpected turn.

Her marriage was suddenly in turmoil. Along with her personal challenges, the organization she worked with for many years began downsizing. Never could she have anticipated such major events, only one of which could have turned her comfortable life into disarray. For a long time, she longed to make sense of it, often asking, "Why this?" "Why me?" "Why now?" and "How will I survive?"

This brings you to the first step of your trip. Check your ticket. It's time to define your problem. Carol had more than one problem, more than one area in her life that was undergoing significant change. Everyone will have at least one issue that is in a state of change, whether it is a child getting up during the night, a corporate merger, a new boss, fluctuating finances, or the desire to shed a few pounds. This is for you and specifically what is important and impacting you today. Your issue may not be as dramatic as my friend's situation to reinvent her career and reshape her expectations of family, or it may be equally as monumental.

Take a moment to define your destination, situation, problem, or issue sufficiently and write down the details on your trip ticket below.

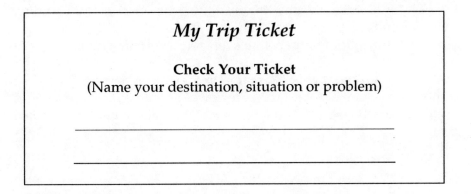

My Trip Ticket

Check Your Ticket
(Name your destination, situation or problem)

We will check in with Carol at the end of the book to see how she fared through her many changes. We'll use a couple of other examples to work through each step of the *Who Packed My Baggage?* process.

Alex just received a promotion based on her technical expertise. She worked well with customers and really loved resolving their problems. She especially enjoyed the technical nature of her job. She loved learning new software applications and finding glitches and fixing them. Most of us would think recognition with a promotion was great, but Alex was not overly comfortable with this. She was more confident handling technical issues, not management, leadership, and personnel issues. In fact, Alex started wondering why they chose her. She didn't believe she had the necessary skills. She didn't think she was as experienced as others, and even went so far as to believe she wasn't worthy of this promotion. Let's pause for a moment, right here and review the Ticket Restriction we all agreed upon. It stated:

My Ticket Restriction

Through the course of my journey, I understand and agree that there will be no putting down, no berating, no judgment, and no criticism of myself or anyone else in any way, shape or form. Liability for loss, delay or damage to my baggage is limited to the price I am willing to pay. This ticket is good for life.

It's important to abide by the restriction to effectively travel through the change process. By unwittingly setting up barriers, by berating, imposing judgment, or by criticizing yourself, others, or the process, you are destined for failure before even getting off the ground.

Alex needs to review this restriction and agree to abide by it before completing step one. After further review, Alex agreed to stop being so hard on herself, look beyond her fears and then complete her trip ticket.

Alex's trip ticket would say:

Alex's Trip Ticket

Check Your Ticket
(Name your destination, situation or problem)

I love my job, I'm not sure I want to leave it and I am

uncomfortable dealing with management issues

Brad finally has some spare time on his day off and wants to work on his model airplanes. He's been waiting to have this opportunity for weeks. His wife Wanda approaches him on that same day and asks for help in the yard, raking leaves, and entertaining their young daughter. Brad had promised to get this work done, so while not an unexpected request, he's also been longing to spend time on his hobby for weeks.

Brad's trip ticket would say:

Brad's Trip Ticket

Check Your Ticket
(Name your destination, situation or problem)

I want to work on my hobby. I don't want to do yard

work.

Like Carol, Alex, and Brad, you will have a situation or question to explore. Now that you know what's come into your life by checking and filling out your ticket, it's time to examine your situation in a hands-on way.

Chapter 4

Step 2: Pack Your Baggage

The baggage you pack is critical to your journey and will contribute to how well you deal with your situation. You may already be flooded with thoughts, feelings, beliefs, and ideas simply by posing your problem and identifying the issues surrounding your journey. All of these reactions are your baggage. To pack your baggage items, you'll need a travel bag.

Use the picture below to represent your travel bag for this journey. To know this is *your* travel bag, take a minute to decorate it with doodles, drawings, words, phrases, colors, stickers, and anything that appeals to you. You are now ready to pack.

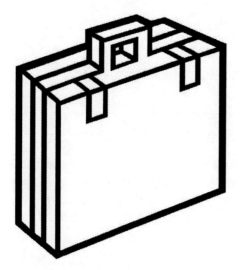

To be sure nothing gets lost during your trip, you have to identify and label your baggage associated with the situation you identified in step one. Consider all the things that you are experiencing or things that are impacting you. Determine all of your thoughts, feelings, beliefs and behaviors in dealing with this issue. Write each one down on the travel tags on the next page. Include anything that comes to mind including your:

- **Thoughts** (I think this situation is stupid, I hate this, I love this, I'm going to fail, I'll manage, I'll die, I can't decide what to do, it's my fault, it's not my fault, how dare they, I'll show them...)

- **Feelings** (I feel scared, I feel angry, I feel happy, I feel resentful, I feel betrayed, I feel guilty, I feel excited, I can't cope...)

- **Beliefs/Values** (I'll have faith, I have no faith, life is unfair, life is too hard, people are basically trustworthy and honest, people can't be trusted, business is corrupt, I believe my boss...)

- **Attitudes/Behaviors** (I deserve more, I deserve less, I'm the best, I'm the worst, everything happens to me, nothing ever works for me, I want revenge, I'll never do it, I can do anything, I'm better than this, out with the old, in with the new...)

- **Relationships** (this may change my relationships with family, friends, boss, co-workers for better or for worse, my relationships may end, there may be new relationships, no one will love me, I have no support, I have good support...)

- **Skills/Knowledge** (I have excellent skills in...[i.e. communication, technology, relationships, negotiation, leadership, management, education], my skills may be outdated, I need to upgrade my skills, you can't teach an old dog new tricks, I have few skills, I'm not smart enough, I'm too educated for this...)

- **Risks** (what if I fail, what if I change, what if I lose financially, what if there is a change in my personal life, my status, my relationships, what if I am not liked, what will happen next...)

- **Gains** (I may be able to let go, I may learn something new, I may be happy, I may grow financially, in my personal life, in status; I may build new relationships, I may succeed, what will happen next...)

- **Other** (other physical, spiritual, emotional, financial impacts...)

Travel Identification Tags

Write down your thoughts, feelings, beliefs, attitudes, and behaviors, knowledge, risks, gains, etc., associated with the situation or problem on your travel identification tags.

Identification Tags	Identification Tags	Identification Tags

Identification Tags	Identification Tags	Identification Tags

Identification Tags	Identification Tags	Identification Tags

Identification Tags	Identification Tags	Identification Tags

Identification Tags	Identification Tags	Identification Tags

Identification Tags	Identification Tags	Identification Tags

For easy reference, list each item you've identified with your travel identification tags onto the Baggage Checklist below.

My Baggage Checklist

Pack Your Baggage
(Identify your thoughts, feelings and beliefs)

Thoughts   _____

                             _____

Feelings   _____

                             _____

Beliefs/Values   _____

                             _____

Attitudes/Behaviors   _____

                             _____

Relationships   _____

                             _____

Knowledge/Skills   _____

                             _____

Risks   _____

                             _____

Gains   _____

                             _____

Other   _____

Once you've completed your Baggage Checklist you're ready to pack. Of course, not all baggage is created equal. Review each item of baggage you've noted on your identification tags, one at a time. Consider whether each thought, feeling, belief, risk, etc., feels light or heavy in weight. For example, identification tags with statements like "I *hate* this situation," or "I have *no* faith," can be negative and limiting. These would be heavy travel items and take a lot of your baggage space. Assess your baggage closely. Even a statement like "I'm the best," or "I have all the skills I need," can be limiting, *if* it closes you to new ideas. These beliefs may prevent you from learning something new. Identification tags with statements like "I'm excited," or "I'll develop new skills," or "I feel rewarded," bring positive energy and with it, opportunities for change and growth. These would weigh less and take less of your baggage space.

If the weight of a baggage item isn't obvious, connect with yourself and feel how your body responds as you consider the item. Is your brow knit together? Are your teeth clenched? Are your lips turned down in a frown or up in a smile? Are your hands open or in tight fists? Are you breathing or holding your breath? Do you feel tightness in your stomach? These responses are signals to the weight of your baggage.

Separate your identification tags into heavy and light baggage. Count how many you have of each. If it takes five positive thoughts, feelings, or beliefs to counter one negative one, we will assume a similar weighting system for your baggage. Assign each light piece of baggage a value of one and each heavy piece of baggage a value of five (it's five times heavier than the lighter baggage). Record the weight of each baggage item on your identification tags or baggage checklist. Add the values of the light and heavy baggage items to determine the total weight of your baggage. For example:

Heavy (negative baggage)	*10 pieces x 5*	*= 50 lbs of heavy baggage*
Light (positive baggage)	*5 pieces x 1*	*= 5 lbs of light baggage*
Total baggage	*50 lbs + 5 lbs*	*= 55 lbs of total baggage*

You are ready to pack your baggage for this trip. To pack your baggage, divide the travel bag below into sections or blocks to represent how you packed. In the example above, your heavy baggage was 50 of the 55 lbs, or most of what you packed. This is how you would divide the total space of your travel bag:

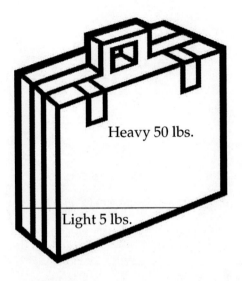

You are now packed and ready to go. One, two, three...lift your travel bag. Remember to bend your knees. Think about the effort it would take to lift and carry around the travel bag with the baggage weight you have just packed. Does your bag need duct tape around it to hold everything inside? Does your bag need wheels to pull the weight behind you? Do you want to lock your bag so no one can see what you are taking along? We will now pack the baggage for our fictitious characters, Alex and Brad.

Alex's baggage:

Light baggage: "I'll make more money," "I have years of technical experience to bring to the role," "This role provides a bigger office with a window," "I'll get an assigned parking space near the building."

Heavy baggage: "I don't want to travel," "I won't be using my technical skills and expertise," "What if my relationships with family and co-workers change," "I'll feel isolated in that big office," "What if I fail and get fired," "The hours will kill my home life," "I don't want fiscal responsibility," "I hate numbers."

Alex's Baggage Checklist

Pack Your Baggage
(Identify your thoughts, feelings and beliefs)

Thoughts	I'll make more money (1) I don't want fiscal responsibility (5)
Feelings	I'll feel isolated(5)
Beliefs/Values	Family is important to me, success is important(2)
Attitudes/Behaviors	I hate human resource work, paperwork(10)
Relationships	I don't want to lose my friends and family(10)
Knowledge/Skills	I have years of technical experience to bring to the role(1)
Risks	Loss of relationships, may fail, be fired (15)
Gains	I get a bigger office and assigned parking (2)

Alex's Baggage—total weight 51 pounds:

Heavy (negative baggage)	*9 pieces x 5*	*= 45 lbs of heavy baggage*
Light (positive baggage)	*6 pieces x 1*	*= 6 lbs of light baggage*
Total baggage	*45 lbs + 6 lbs*	*= 51 lbs of total baggage*

Alex's Travel Bag:

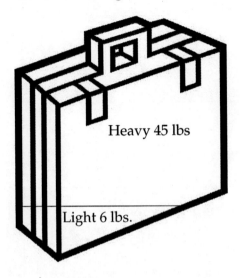

Heavy 45 lbs

Light 6 lbs.

Brad's baggage:

Light baggage: "I have a day off."

Heavy baggage: "I'm angry that I won't get to work on my hobby," "I resent Wanda for not discussing this plan with me," "I won't have any self time," "I don't feel like I'm a priority around here."

Brad's Baggage Checklist

Pack Your Baggage
(Identify your thoughts, feelings and beliefs)

Thoughts   I have a day off (1)

Feelings   I am angry, I am resentful (10)

Beliefs/Values   I am not appreciated (5), I love working on my

                    hobby (1)

Attitudes/Behavior Blaming behavior towards my wife (5)

Relationships   Strained relationship with wife and daughter (5)

Knowledge/Skills   _____

Risks   Family dysfunction, blaming, arguing, hurting others

                    (5) no self time (5)

Gains   _____

Brad's Baggage—total weight 37 pounds:

Heavy (negative baggage)	*7 pieces x 5*	*= 35 lbs of heavy baggage*
Light (positive baggage)	*2 pieces x 1*	*= 2 lbs of light baggage*
Total baggage	*35 lbs + 2 lbs*	*= 37 lbs of total baggage*

Brad's Travel Bag:

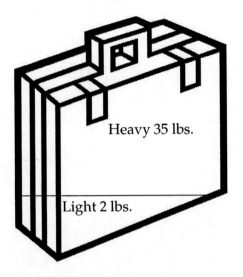

Heavy 35 lbs.

Light 2 lbs.

Optional Exercise:

This is an optional exercise we do in workshops. If you want to physically experience packing your travel bag, this exercise allows you to expand the process. It's fun and easy.

First design your travel bag. This can be an envelope, gift bag, paper bag, or box. Choose something that appeals to you and can be used to pack your baggage for your situation. Make this travel bag your own by decorating it with crayons, markers, pastels, stickers, ribbons, whatever you enjoy.

To give weight to the baggage you identified on your baggage checklist, gather some light objects like paper clips, beads, or cotton balls, and some heavy objects like marbles, stones or coins. Separate your baggage identification tags into heavy and light baggage. Count how many you have of each. Place a corresponding number of marbles, stones, or coins for your heavy baggage and place paper clips, beads, or cotton balls for your light baggage, into the travel bag you've created.

Remember to use five marbles, stones, or coins for each heavy baggage item and one paper clip, bead, or cotton ball, for every light baggage item. By lifting this travel bag you will have a greater appreciation for the weight of your thoughts, feelings, beliefs, and behaviors.

Chapter 5

Step 3: Claim Your Lost Baggage

For this part of your trip, you will assess the baggage you packed in step 2. Claiming your lost baggage is key to how well you will deal with your situation. During your trip through change, you have the opportunity to stop along the way to find any of your lost or forgotten baggage.

On most trips I've taken, I invariably find I've forgotten to pack something, left an important item at home, or wish I'd brought along something different. Are you happy traveling to your change destination with your baggage? How easy is it to lift your travel bag? How much does your baggage weigh? Does it feel light or heavy? Will your baggage fit in a compact carry-on bag or will you need a trunk with three locks and a chain and a baggage cart to hold everything you've packed for this trip? Is there room for more or is your baggage bulging at the seams with every possibility? Will the ticket agent charge you extra for the limiting beliefs and negative thoughts you've packed? Can you afford to pay the extra price to your well-being for your baggage?

If you think you can afford to pay extra for your baggage, you may want to pause and consider the real emotional, physical, and spiritual price. How will the stress of negative thoughts and feelings impact your physical and emotional health? How will resistance to upgrading your skills, forgiving someone, surrendering to your situation, changing roles or organizations affect you, your loved ones, and your future? Do you want to feel like this? How long can you hold out? Would you rather take that eight-week night course to learn how to effectively use the new software program at work or struggle and feel frustrated each time you need to compile information or run a report, wasting time and energy? Does it make sense to hang on to anger about a senseless or hurtful comment made by a co-worker or friend, or to express your discomfort and needs or simply let it go? Do you really have to go it alone after a painful break-up or will you let go of your pride and seek support and guidance to work through a challenging emotional period in your life? How has your baggage worked for you so far?

If you're not willing to pay any price for your baggage and prefer to pack light for this change, it's time to look at old, worn out beliefs, antiquated skills, harmful relationships, self deprecating thoughts, and negative attitudes to make room and replace them with the new ones you want and need for the success of your change trip.

Go through your baggage checklist again. Choose the thoughts, feelings, beliefs, attitudes, relationships, skills, risks, and anything else you want to modify or leave behind. This doesn't have to be difficult. It can be as simple as taming negatives like "I *can't*," or "I *won't*," by changing them to "I *can*," and "I *will*." It may be as easy as reframing fear and anxiety into excitement and anticipation. For example, reframe a thought like, "This is the first time I've flown and I'm anxious about what could happen," to "I've never flown before and I'm so excited about finally getting out of town." Or "I'm really scared about losing my job over this merger," to "I believe this merger will provide me with an opportunity to expand my planning and management skills or find a new vocation," or "I'm going to use this lay-off to go back to school and do what I've always wanted."

Change a long held belief about yourself or others and proclaim a new one. Become "I'm worthy, open and ready to learn," rather than "You can't teach an old dog new tricks." Pluck out your gray negative thoughts like "This relationship makes me unhappy," and replace them with colorful positive ones like "I'll expect and will only accept something healthy and happy."

Consider other options for each piece of your heavy baggage. Massage and turn these thoughts, feelings, and beliefs into positives. If you feel hesitant, it may be a sign that you need to move something out of the way in order to move on. Don't let this stop you from claiming your lost baggage. Even if you are skeptical at first, list new lighter thoughts, feelings, beliefs, behaviors and more, on your lost baggage list.

Lost Baggage List

Claim Your Lost Baggage
(Consider your other options)

Thoughts   _____

Feelings   _____

Beliefs/Values   _____

Attitudes/Behaviors   _____

Relationships   _____

Knowledge/Skills   _____

Risks   _____

Gains   _____

Other   _____

Remove the old non-essential baggage items you've decided to leave behind and their corresponding weights. Write out new travel tags with the lost or forgotten baggage that you have now claimed. Determine the new weight of your baggage using the value of five for heavy baggage and the value of one for light baggage and repack your travel bag.

Represent how you've repacked on the travel bag below:

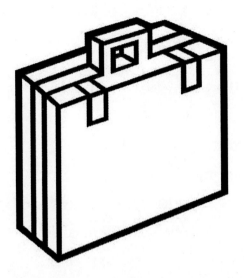

Lift your travel bag again. It should now contain only the new and essential baggage you chose to take along for your journey. Can you feel a difference? Are you happier with what you've packed? What are your expectations now? Are there still areas of baggage you could change? If so, you may want to decide whether this baggage is necessary or if you can live without it.

Alex and Brad reclaimed their lost baggage with these results:

Alex's lost baggage:

"I'll have management status, perks, and bigger bonuses;" "It's an opportunity to learn new leadership, communication, and management skills;" "This is recognition I've worked for and aspired to;" "I have years of technical experience to bring to this new role;" "My family and friends are supportive;" "The staff respect me;" "I love to feel like a student;" "I can learn how to set different priorities and find balance in my work and home life."

Alex's Lost Baggage List

Claim Your Lost Baggage
(Consider your other options)

Thoughts	Recognition I've always wanted (1)
Feelings	I am proud (1), I am excited (1)
Beliefs/Values	I value having the opportunity to be a student(1)
	I learn to set priorities (1), learn to balance life (1)
Attitudes/Behaviors	Positive attitude (1), reframing for the positive(1)
Relationships	Family loves/supports me (1), Friends support me(1)
Knowledge/Skills	Learn new leadership (1), communication (1) and
	management (1) skills, years of experience I bring (1)
Risks	
Gains	Perks (1), bonuses (1), management status (1)
Other	

Alex removed 35 lbs. of heavy negatives and replaced them with 17 lbs. of lighter positives. She found that this heavy baggage didn't work for her change trip: not wanting to learn human resource work (5 lbs.), paperwork (5 lbs.), not wanting to lose friends and family—they said they support her (10 lbs.), fear of failure or of being fired—she is accepting the opportunity to learn, grow and prioritize (10 lbs.), not wanting fiscal responsibility—she is willing to grow (5 lbs.).

Alex looked through her situation again, reframed the negatives, looked for and found the positives, the silver linings, and was able to change the weight of her baggage from 51 lbs. to 33 lbs., making this trip a lot more manageable, with opportunities for growth and learning and maybe even some fun. She's replacing outworn and limiting baggage, with light positive thoughts, behaviors, and actions.

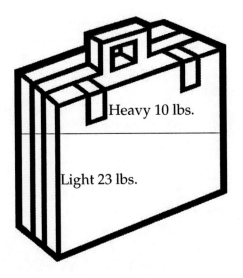

Heavy 10 lbs.

Light 23 lbs.

Brad's lost baggage:

Brad had difficulty identifying and reclaiming lost baggage. Rather than use the opportunity to examine his thoughts, feelings, and attitudes more closely, Brad turned his frustration about his issue into blame towards his wife Wanda, proclaiming it was her fault he was in this position.

Were it not for Wanda and her demands, Brad felt he would be having a great time working on his project, just as he'd intended. Brad has forgotten the one important restriction to his trip through change. Let's review it again as a reminder:

My Ticket Restriction

Through the course of my journey, I understand and agree that there will be no putting down, no berating, no judgment, and no criticism of myself or anyone else in any way, shape or form. Liability for loss, delay or damage to my baggage is limited to the price I am willing to pay. This ticket is good for life.

By choosing to blame Wanda, Brad is missing out on the opportunity to be responsible for his own decisions and the quality of his experience. Being fully accountable for his actions is empowering and essential. Brad decided that being responsible and accountable was far better than feeling out of control of his life.

After further exploration, Brad was able to declare his lost baggage:

"I'll have family time," "I can get some much needed physical exercise," "I have pride in my home," "We can work together as a team and finish quickly," "I'll have a sense of accomplishment," "I will keep my word and commitment," "I have an opportunity to learn to communicate my needs more clearly to my wife," "I can learn to plan better with my family by prioritizing activities on my days off."

Brad's Lost Baggage List

Claim Your Lost Baggage
(Consider your other options)

Thoughts	Thinking positively about the situation (1)
Feelings	Feelings of pride (1) and accomplishment (1)
Beliefs/Values	More quality family time (1), keeping commitments (1)
Attitudes/Behaviors	Cooperative behavior (1) and attitude (1)
Relationships	Building closer familial relationships (1)
Knowledge/Skills	
Risks	
Gains	Physical exercise (1), opportunity to strengthen communication skills (1)
Other	

When Brad was willing to examine his situation more closely, he was able to manage change in a positive way. He was able to change his resentful and angry feelings (10 lbs.), alter his blaming behavior towards his wife (5 lbs.), focus on quality family time and follow through on commitments (5 lbs.) instead of focusing on believing he was unappreciated (5 lbs.). He was also able to help heal family dysfunction (5 lbs.). The one thing he has not yet found time for is his hobby. He is committed to better planning of his days off with his family in the future.

With all the positive changes, Brad has added 10 items worth 10 lbs. to his light baggage and has lost 30 lbs. representing most of the heavy baggage. His new baggage now weighs only 17 pounds. This is significantly lighter than the original 37 pounds of baggage he was going to carry around for his situation. Brad has improved the quality of his trip today by taking the time to explore his issues and by choosing responses that were positive and fulfilling.

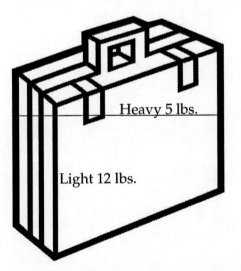

In searching for your lost or forgotten baggage, it may be that you feel a need to hold on to certain thoughts, beliefs, people, etc. You may not be in the best space or be ready to let go of a concern or to receive a particular lesson. This delay may simply be a part of your growth and development to come at a later time and different place. This is to be expected and is a part of any change process. You can always come back to these issues later in your trip if you choose. Or you may want to stop and restate the nature of your trip, evaluate your baggage one more time, and pack again.

Optional Exercise:

As a continuation of the optional exercise you began in chapter 4, you can repack the real travel bag you designed. Remove your old, non-essential baggage identification tags and their corresponding heavy weights (marbles, stones, or coins). Pack again using new identification tags or a new baggage checklist with the lost baggage you claimed. Find out the new weight of your baggage using the value system of five for heavy baggage and one for light baggage. Your travel bag should now contain the essential baggage for your situation. Lift it again. Can you feel a difference?

Chapter 6

Step 4: Choose Your Fare

One of the positive benefits of a journey to a destination of change is that you have the power and the ability to choose your fare and whether it will be a first class, economy, or bargain trip. The fare you choose will also determine where you put your energy and resources. By understanding the qualities in each fare for a trip towards change, you can decide how you will treat yourself and how others will treat you during your experience:

First Class Change

- Advance boarding before the crowds (You are aware of the opportunities presented by change and know what you need to do to succeed.)
- Front of the line (You are able to experience and savor the positive aspects of a change while others are still contemplating or complaining.)
- First choice from a full menu (You are empowered and can choose where to give your energy and the quality of energy you want to receive.)
- Room to stretch and breathe (You see the options available to you and the opportunities for growth and learning.)
- Quality service (You respect yourself and others respect you and acknowledge your positive attitude and efforts.)
- A seat is always available (There will be a place for you in any situation because you are prepared and empowered.)

- Happy and calm (You own your change experience and relax in your understanding that change happens for a reason.)
- Great seat assignment (There is no better place than up front to experience the excitement of something new.)
- Great view (Location is everything and you have a front row seat where you can clearly see to identify and manage any obstacles in your path.)

In first class the focus is positively centered on the opportunity for growth and development for yourself and others. It's about taking personal responsibility for your attitude and having the confidence that you can manage any obstacles and overcome barriers. There is a high level of trust inside with yourself and outside with the people around you. You know you can develop the skills you need, that you have the ability to communicate your needs and intentions, you can ask for help and admit shortcomings or mistakes, take care of yourself, make wise choices and move forward.

Economy Change

- Wait for your turn to board (You may sit on the fence waiting to see how the change goes for those in first class and bargain sale before making up your mind.)
- You are anxious about taking off and landing (You sense things are changing and may choose not to make any moves until the situation seems stable and you can assess things more.)
- Middle seat assignment (You know there's opportunity for the better but you're willing to settle for less, you see this as time to process and evaluate the risks and benefits for you.)
- Some choice is still available from the menu (You are aware the changes are occurring around you and you need and want to find your place one way or the other.)
- Less space to move around (You have options but may feel limited by your unwillingness to make choices and to act.)
- Some comfort in economy (You don't have to commit one way or the other, positively or negatively through change.)

- Far from the toilets (You're in a place where you have time to process what is needed to go into first class or bargain class and you could be convinced of one fare or the other if you can see what's in it for you.)
- You need to ring for service to be noticed (Acknowledgement and focus may seem elusive and may seem to be going to others.)

With economy class you understand that opportunities exist, but you are more conscious of the obstacles. Here you may feel hesitancy and reluctance to take the risks associated with personal or professional change. Though you may harbor less than positive feelings about the situation, you are dedicated to remaining professional with the understanding that the situation is part of your job or your life and you do have certain obligations.

Bargain Sale Change

- Back of the line (Everyone else is way ahead of you in accepting and working with the change and they seem to be managing and thriving without you.)
- Last to get on board (Everyone is celebrating their successes by the time you arrive.)
- You can't be heard over the engines (No one will hear your complaints about the change; they are all too busy enjoying their first class change experience.)
- Motion sickness (You may feel queasy with the lack of control you are feeling.)
- Squeezed into a narrow middle seat (It's difficult to change your position about change when you can't see ahead and there's nothing to go back to.)
- Right beside the toilets (You need to pull yourself away from the downward, spinning vortex of despair.)
- Peanuts or pretzels (All the good opportunities will be snatched up. Being so far in back, all you have to choose from are the remnants of those who have gone before you. If you don't step up to the challenge of change, others will get the window seats, the best office space, the most interesting projects, a perfect partner, or a promotion.)

The focus in bargain class is negative and you don't keep this a secret. You feel hard done by or passed over and everyone is going to hear about it and know it. Here you'll experience outright complaining, flat out anger, and a good dose of righteousness. You're mired in the muck and your focus is on living and reporting the bad news. You believe there is no opportunity and that everything is an obstacle. You feel it can't be done, feel used, abused and unappreciated by everyone else and the system, and you don't want to look at your energy flow to try something new or different. Why bother, nothing ever changes in the end anyway, right?

Once you've chosen where you want to put your energy for your trip, fill out the fare section of your trip ticket. Keep the descriptions of each fare in mind. Review the choices you made in packing and claiming your lost baggage. Your baggage will impact the fare you choose. Think about the actions you'll have to take to qualify for each fare. Be honest with yourself. This is not about writing down the *right* answer. It's about what's real for you.

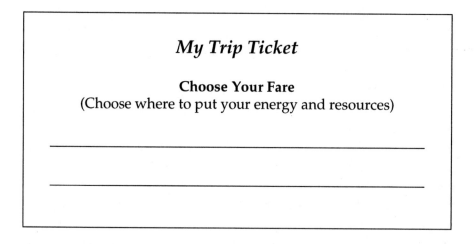

My Trip Ticket

Choose Your Fare
(Choose where to put your energy and resources)

_____

_____

Alex and Brad have chosen their fares.

Alex's Fare:

Alex has become aware of: her work environment (she is paying attention to it), options she now sees, new attitudes and behaviors she can adopt, and steps to take to upgrade and learn new skills. She can now ask herself whether she will plan or just let things happen. She can also consider expressing her needs and concerns to management. She may request their support in her professional growth (mentoring, education, funding, etc.). Alex is acknowledging her situation and moving ahead. This is first class travel.

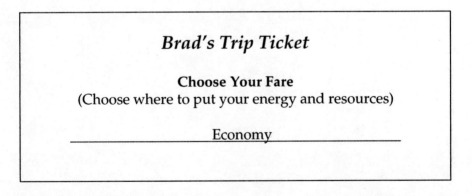

Alex's Trip Ticket

Choose Your Fare
(Choose where to put your energy and resources)

First Class

Brad's Fare:

Brad has become aware of: his own limiting attitudes and behaviors with his family, but he continues to have difficulty expressing his needs and is unable to set personal boundaries.

Brad's Trip Ticket

Choose Your Fare
(Choose where to put your energy and resources)

Economy

He'd like to communicate openly with his wife but is held back by a fear of appearing selfish. If he puts himself first what will his wife and daughter think? Will they criticize or blame him? Brad's challenge is to learn how to speak up for himself and to set healthy boundaries.

Everything can and will get done with careful planning and open communication about priorities. Brad needs to take care of himself in order to take care of his family. Brad is still exhibiting reluctance and resentment and has chosen economy travel. He may have to experience more discomfort before he's ready to take the next steps to first class. In order to get the things that are meaningful to him, he may need to change the quality of his relationship.

To the credit of Alex and Brad, they have chosen to avoid bargain fares, where they would stay stuck with no desire to learn and grow from their situations. People in bargain fare are happy complaining, feeling unrecognized, and have no desire to move forward. They are unwilling to accept their personal power and ability to choose something more.

If you treat yourself in a first-class way through change, you'll receive the same level of positive energy in return. If the bargain sale fare is your choice, that's fine right now too. It may help to bring along a bag lunch to provide you with the extra calories for the additional energy you will be expending to support your choice.

Chapter 7

Step 5: Make Your Connections

You have now packed a lighter travel bag by identifying the essentials necessary for your trip and the non-essentials that you can leave behind. In creating your itinerary, you have assessed each step and the choices you've made. You will arrive safely at your ultimate destination if you are also able to make your connections along the way. Recognize that first class travel may also mean being willing to learn as you go, see things in a new way, grow from challenges, or find the opportunities in mistakes. Just like making travel connections, some lessons and personal growth will be more challenging and take longer than others.

It's important to evaluate what you have learned and what works and doesn't work during your experiences. Delays do occur for a reason and they can have costs and benefits. This doesn't mean that bad things won't ever happen. It does mean that you will know the truth about your situation and be able to create a positive place in your life to deal with the issues that do come your way.

You may need to take the time to upgrade your skills (a short course, night school, 3 years at college); build a better support system (social network, classmates, counselor, financial consultant, church group, a 12-step program, clubs or activities with like-minded individuals); or practice healthy behaviors (anger management, listening skills, parenting, gratitude, conflict resolution, negotiation). All of these things take time. These are excellent connections on your way to first class change.

Identify your resistance, concerns, and lessons and elaborate on whether each will help or impede your progress. You may be resistant to the feelings you are experiencing (loss, anger, pain, fear). You may be concerned about your financial future, your relationships, physical or emotional state, or your skills and abilities. These very things may prompt you to view situations differently, learn new responses, change beliefs, behaviors, or upgrade skills, so you can make the best of change.

Think about how you are going to proceed. Are you stopped, stalled, or moving straight ahead? What are the obstacles? Why are they there? Is there another way around them? How much energy are you willing to give these? Are you finding opportunities to learn and grow along the way? Are you willing to pursue these opportunities? What will work and what won't work? Embrace something you can't control. The opportunity may be to let go, to remember your strengths or to simply give your best.

Here are some specific questions that may help guide you through this step:

1. *What can you learn from the travel bag you packed in steps 2 and 3 by looking at the quality (negatives/positives) and quantity (number/weight) of baggage (time/energy) you put into this situation?*
2. *What areas would you like or need to experience less during your trip?*
3. *What areas would you like or need to experience more during your trip?*
4. *Look at your travel bag for future opportunities for growth and development. What can you learn from your baggage and the way you packed?*
5. *Identify at least three things you can make room for in your travel bag (lost or new thoughts, feelings, beliefs, behaviors, skills, etc.).*

Fill out your trip ticket with the opportunities for learning and growth that you can take advantage of in dealing with your situation. Once again, be as honest as you can with yourself. Include everything, especially if it may stretch and expand your usual comfort zone.

My Trip Ticket

Make Your Connections
(Find opportunities for your learning and growth)

_____

_____

_____

_____

_____

_____

_____

_____

Alex and Brad make their connections:

Alex's Connections:

1. Alex learned her heavy baggage was keeping her from learning the skills necessary to confidently take on her new role.
2. Alex decided she wanted to let go of her fears and stop stagnating. She was afraid to let go of her old job. It was comfortable and she was an expert.
3. Alex wanted to focus more on growing, learning, and achieving her full potential.

4. She had opportunities to openly communicate with her employer, to develop new relationships with her co-workers and new peers, and to become a student again, which was something she loved.

5. She made room for renewed confidence, for progressing personally, professionally and financially, and for new skills.

Alex's Trip Ticket

Make Your Connections
(Find opportunities for your learning and growth)

Heavy baggage will not keep me from learning skills necessary to

confidently take on a new role

This is a time to focus on growth and learning to reach my potential

Pursue the opportunities to openly communicate with my employer

Develop new relationships with my co-workers and new peers

Brad's Connections:

1. Brad recognized his anger and fears when he didn't communicate his priorities and boundaries.

2. Brad would like to deal less with his negative reactions to his family.

3. Brad wants to feel happy about the time he spends at home and feel more in control of his time.

4. Brad has the opportunity to learn to communicate effectively, find balance, and be empowered.

5. He can make room to prioritize and plan his time to meet both his personal and family commitments, to openly express his needs, and to learn to reframe his situations positively by taking responsibility for his choices.

Brad's Trip Ticket

Make Your Connections
(Find opportunities for your learning and growth)

Recognize anger and fears when I don't communicate

Feel happy about the time I spend at home

Feel more in control of my time

Learn to communicate more effectively

Find balance by prioritizing and planning

Reframe situations positively by taking responsibility

_____

You can try to run from change, but it will run right along beside you, keeping pace positively or negatively, light or heavy, first class or bargain. It's not personal. If you can get past obstacles and challenges, you can feel good about yourself and everything around you and be content. Think about how you want to arrive at your destination and what the result will be of the itinerary you have created. The outcome is truly your decision.

Chapter 8

Step 6: Arrive At Your Destination

Arriving at your destination can be so glorious and wonderful that you may never want it to change. Enjoy the opportunity to savor the result, experience it, and revel in it. Celebrate your success, you worked for it, you deserve it. Other times the outcome can be challenging and even painful. You may not like the result of the baggage you packed and the fare you chose. If it's not the result you desire, ask yourself whether it is truly negative or if it's really where you want or need to be right now. Did the outcome you want actually change without you being aware? Did you make all the necessary connections along the way (knowledge, relationships, support systems, etc.)? Did you evaluate a realistic estimated time of arrival? Were you delayed or unwilling to take risks or were you rerouted by blaming others or from your own beliefs? Were you honest with yourself?

To complete the final piece of your trip ticket, describe what it means to finally arrive at your destination. Define the outcome you will achieve with all the steps you've taken.

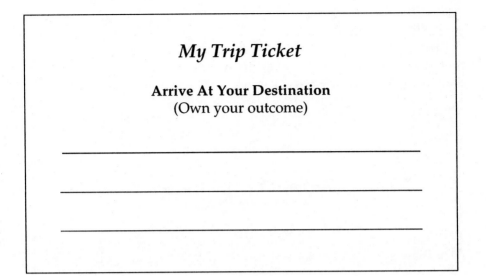

How do you like the trip you've created for yourself? Now that you've made plans for your journey, how does it feel? Is there a decision or choice you'd like to change? Is there anything you would do differently? What would you want the outcome to be instead? Are there experiences that may at first seem negative and actually be opportunities? Go back over your trip and focus on all the things you did get from your journey. Find the silver linings.

The outcome may not match your expectations and you may not get exactly what you want. You may still have to deal with a lay-off, a broken relationship, or a difficult boss. You can't control change. What you can control are your reactions to change and the experience you choose to create. Only you know what you want the situation to look like and feel like and when and how you will arrive at your outcome. Alex and Brad arrive at their destinations.

Alex's arrival:

Alex's trip began with uncertainty and ambivalence. She didn't know if the new job was right for her and if it was worth the risks. Once she made plans for the changes she was more comfortable with her choice and confident in her ability to learn. Having fully processed the risks and benefits that came with the opportunity, Alex wouldn't change a thing. The outcome is what she wanted: more money, perks, bonuses, new skills, learning how to communicate at a different level, and feeling like a student again. Although some of these seemed negative at first, (leaving peers, more travel, change in skills), upon further evaluation, Alex knew these were really blessings in disguise.

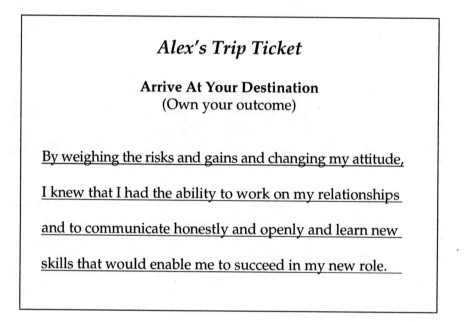

Alex's Trip Ticket

Arrive At Your Destination
(Own your outcome)

By weighing the risks and gains and changing my attitude,

I knew that I had the ability to work on my relationships

and to communicate honestly and openly and learn new

skills that would enable me to succeed in my new role.

Brad's arrival:

Brad's trip began with strong reactions and feelings to his situation, including blaming others. He felt encouraged when he realized he had options and could make changes, should he choose. Because he decided to travel economy (by delaying communication of his needs), Brad knew there was more to learn in setting boundaries with his family and taking care of himself. Brad felt more positive in working with the family because he was able to reframe the nature of their activity (from a chore to quality family time). While this was helpful in working through this situation, Brad still had an opportunity to build his confidence and improve his communication skills and relationships.

Brad's Trip Ticket

Arrive At Your Destination
(Own your outcome)

I'm satisfied with how this situation turned out.

I know I'm responsible for my thoughts and actions.

I still need to work on my relationships at home,

setting priorities and finding more balance in my life.

I still have work to do and that's okay.

Remember Carol from the beginning of the book? Carol's life changed dramatically after her marriage ended and the company she worked for went through downsizing. After focusing on her "bad" luck for over a year, feeling sorry for herself, unloved and unappreciated, one day she found she no longer had the energy to support her negative beliefs. These beliefs were exhausting her mentally and physically and were impacting her relationships, her health, and the quality of her work. Carol finally chose to step back, take her time and work through her baggage by finding out what was really important to her and how she wanted to live.

Carol took a number of important steps. She decided her relationship failed because *it* did, not because she did. She took the time to rebuild her support system, began an exercise program and took classes in things she had only thought about: cooking, writing, golf. She focused on self-improvement and her new child and worked hard for the company she was with. She was rewarded with self-acceptance, forgiveness for her ex-husband, unconditional love for her daughter, the friends who stayed beside her, and the new friends she made along the way. Carol was also the beneficiary of two promotions, more money, and, after a few practice runs, she found a new, deeper, committed relationship. Carol's life didn't change over night. It took understanding and dedication to the process of change and time.

The secret to managing change can be found in the process of assessing each step and making choices. This means being responsible for the manner in which you arrive at your destination and the outcome of the situation. Whatever the result, positive, negative, or something in between, always remember the question, "Who Packed My Baggage?" Even if you're not at the exact destination you had hoped for, celebrate the fact that you've come this far and also savor the accomplishment of starting the process. That alone takes courage and effort. You will always have ample opportunities to develop your packing skills and hone your ability to manage change. Your willingness to find a positive way to deal with change and take responsibility will keep your baggage light, your trips pleasant, and you empowered, each step of the way. **Congratulations!**

Chapter 9

Who Packed My Baggage? Travel Itinerary

You've made all the choices, managed your trip and created your own travel itinerary for change. You've done it, well done! Let's take another look at all the steps that you, Alex, and Brad have accomplished:

Step 1: **Check Your Ticket**
You've named your destination, situation, or problem

Step 2: **Pack Your Baggage**
You've identified your thoughts, feelings, and beliefs

Step 3: **Claim Your Lost Baggage**
You've considered all your options

Step 4: **Choose Your Fare**
You've decided where to put your energy and resources

Step 5: **Make Your Connections**
You've found your opportunities for learning and personal growth

Step 6: **Arrive At Your Destination**
You've owned your outcome

By practicing and applying this six-step approach, you will be empowered when it comes to change. You can make excuses or have results as you build a travel itinerary for any change. It's your choice. You now have the tools to understand, accept, and foster the environment in which you will create the changes in your life. Alex and Brad completed their full travel itineraries.

Alex's Travel Itinerary

Ticket: Situation	leaving technical job for new management role
Baggage: Thoughts/ Feelings/Beliefs	fears of failure, leaving co-workers, travel
	long hours, not having sufficient skills, no
	longer being an expert, more money, office
Lost Baggage: Other Options	excitement, challenge, perks, new skills, love of learning
Fare: Energy/Resources	First Class
Connections: Lessons	opportunity to learn, practice personal and professional
	balance, change and grow new relationships, new
	communication skills
Destination: Outcome	comfort with my choice and confidence in my abilities
Other	open to new challenges and future changes

In response to the question, "Who Packed My Baggage?" I agree that I have packed, planned and approved my Itinerary for this journey. I accept that I am solely responsible for the quality of my travel experience including the weight of my baggage, fare of my trip, making my connections, and the safe arrival at my destination.

_____   _____
Date   Signature

My Ticket Restriction
Through the course of my journey, I understand and agree that there will be no putting down, no berating, no judgment, and no criticism of myself or anyone else in any way, shape or form. Liability for loss, delay or damage to my baggage is limited to the price I am willing to pay. This ticket is good for life.

Brad's Travel Itinerary

Ticket: Situation	work on hobby, not do yard work
Baggage: Thoughts/ Feelings/Beliefs	anger, resentment, feeling selfish, unappreciated, blaming
Lost Baggage: Other Options	joy, family connection, love, exercise, accomplishment
Fare: Energy/Resources	economy
Connections: Lessons	need to set priorities, learn to reframe meaning of tasks, opportunity to communicate more clearly
Destination: Outcome	accountable for my choices, feelings of encouragement and opportunity to build loving relationships while taking care of myself
Other:	more self time

In response to the question, "Who Packed My Baggage?" I agree that I have packed, planned and approved my Itinerary for this journey. I accept that I am solely responsible for the quality of my travel experience including the weight of my baggage, fare of my trip, making my connections, and the safe arrival at my destination.

_____   _____

Date   Signature

My Ticket Restriction
Through the course of my journey, I understand and agree that there will be no putting down, no berating, no judgment, and no criticism of myself or anyone else in any way, shape or form. Liability for loss, delay or damage to my baggage is limited to the price I am willing to pay. This ticket is good for life.

Packing for change doesn't have to be time consuming or difficult. With practice, you can quickly assess any situation, weigh and review your baggage, choose lighter alternatives and attitudes, find the opportunities to learn and grow, decide where to put your valuable energy and resources, and invest in a positive outcome. A travel itinerary for your future change trips and a travel bag with a summary of all the tools you've learned can be found at the end of this chapter. Keep this on hand. Cut it out, copy it, write it down and display it somewhere close by. Use this tool to your advantage and the next time you ask, "Who Packed My Baggage?" you will gladly know it wasn't your spouse, parent, sibling, friend, boss, co-worker, sales clerk, customer service agent, neighbor, or a stranger on the street. You can proudly proclaim a resounding, ME!

Who Packed My Baggage?

Travel Itinerary

Ticket: Situation   _____

Baggage: Thoughts   _____
Feelings/Beliefs
                            _____

Lost Baggage: _____
Other Options
                            _____

Fare: Energy/   _____
Resources

Connections: Lessons   _____

                            _____

Destination: Outcome   _____

In response to the question, "Who Packed My Baggage?" I agree that I have packed, planned and approved my Itinerary for this journey. I accept that I am solely responsible for the quality of my travel experience including the weight of my baggage, fare of my trip, making my connections, and the safe arrival at my destination.

_____   _____
Date   Signature

My Ticket Restriction
Through the course of my journey, I understand and agree that there will be no putting down, no berating, no judgment, and no criticism of myself or anyone else in any way, shape or form. Liability for loss, delay or damage to my baggage is limited to the price I am willing to pay. This ticket is good for life.

©Cat Langdon 2004

Who Packed My Baggage?

Travel Bag

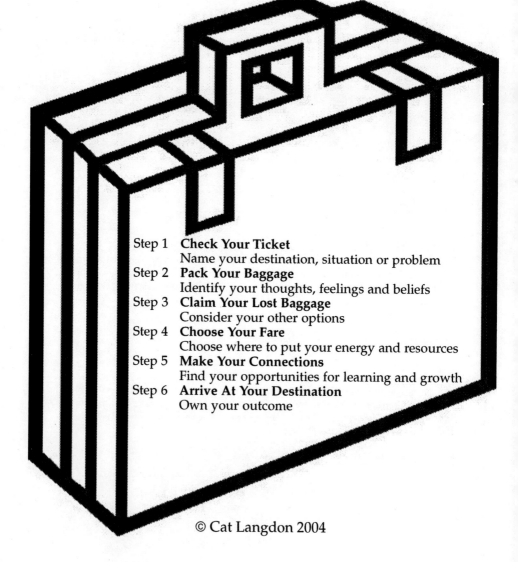

Step 1 **Check Your Ticket**
Name your destination, situation or problem
Step 2 **Pack Your Baggage**
Identify your thoughts, feelings and beliefs
Step 3 **Claim Your Lost Baggage**
Consider your other options
Step 4 **Choose Your Fare**
Choose where to put your energy and resources
Step 5 **Make Your Connections**
Find your opportunities for learning and growth
Step 6 **Arrive At Your Destination**
Own your outcome

© Cat Langdon 2004

*"Through change I can see
more of what I can be."*

—Cat Langdon

About the Author

Cat Langdon is a leader with over 20 years of experience in the public and private sectors. Cat has experience in facilitation, conflict resolution, team building, customer service, communication and managing change. Cat is Co-founder of Inspire Communications Unlimited, an organization that promotes personal and professional growth and development.

0-595-31449-X

Printed in the United Kingdom
by Lightning Source UK Ltd.
109401UKS00002B/301-303